Furry, Feathered & Finned

amazing & amusing animal abc's

story by megs thompson – illustrations by liz k

Furry, Feathered & Finned

amazing & amusing animal abc's

is a work of my own creation.

ISBN - 978-1-961185-17-3 (paperback)
ISBN - 978-1-961185-19-7 (ebook)

story by megs thompson - www.megswrites.com

illustrations by liz k - www.fiverr.com/s/z6VAqz

in omnia paratus publishing
www.inomniaparatuspublishing.com

this story is dedicated to you;

the grown-ups & future grown-ups who aren't afraid to have fun, sing off key, dance in the rain & let your imagination run wild.

—m

Letters are fun,
and animals too.
But not all cool animals,
live in the zoo.

So cuddle up close,
and keep your eyes bright.
We're about to meet creatures,
that can be a real sight.

Some of these creatures
live under the sea.
While others prefer,
garbage cans and alleys.

Some may sound made-up,
created for fun.
But who knows if they're real,
until you've seen one.

A is for Angry Stinging Desert Rat.

With teeth so sharp & a tail so fast.

This way & that way, they creep through the sand,

So watch where you're walking in their hot homeland.

B is for Bear Cats, in bamboo they climb,
Black and white fuzzballs, just taking their time.
Giants so gentle always hanging around,
Keep your eyes to the sky & not on the ground.

C is for City Chicks, sometimes they fly,
Between tall sky scrapers & cars rushing by.
On bustling sidewalks they flock as a gang,
Their feathers ruffling as they shake off the rain.

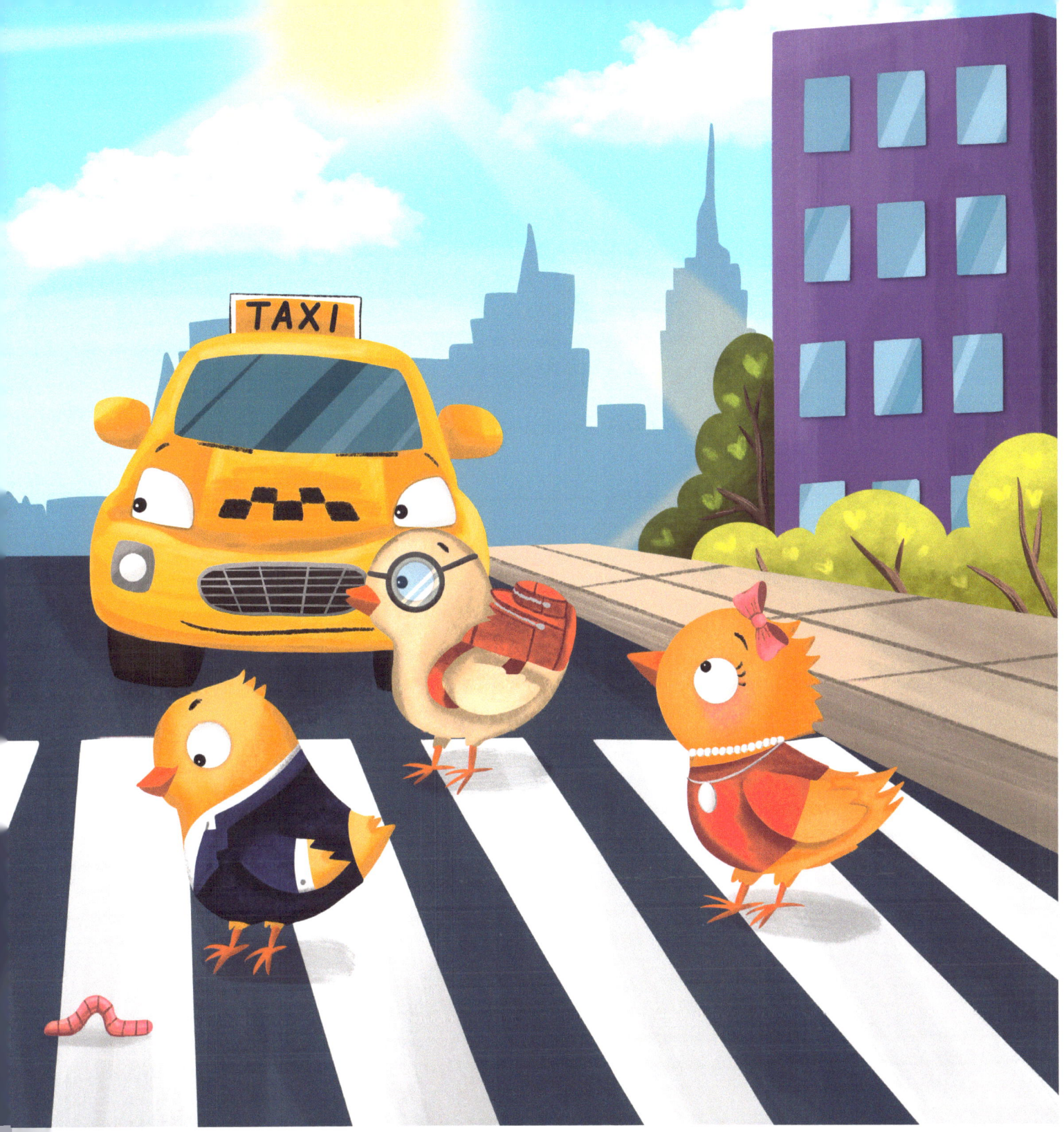

D is for Dangerous Pancakes with jam,

Flipped into the ocean from hot frying pans.

With tails of bacon that sizzle & sting,

Keep your eyes peeled wide whenever you swim.

E is for Energized Flitters with wings,
The tiniest creatures that buzz when they sing.
With colors so bright, they zip through the sky,
Never pausing to give a thought as to their why.

F is for Fancy Turkeys, dripping in jewels,

They're pretty to look at but mean as a rule.

With colors so bright, they strut and display,

But whatever you do, just stay out of their way.

G is for Gigantic Water Chickens that honk,
They hang out in lakes, creeks, rivers & swamps.
With wings spread wide, they fly high in the sky,
Screaming off key together as they pass by.

H is for Hopping Floofs with big ears & feet,
Playing in gardens with carrots to eat.
With noses & tails that twitch as they hop,
Sometimes it may seem like they'll never stop.

I is for Iceberg Loafers with paws,

They nap on the snow, eating fish they catch, raw.

In their frozen home, they roam & explore,

Floating in the ocean, without any oars.

J is for Junk Food Burglars with masks.

They'll snatch up your pizza, never thinking to ask.

If you're near the beach, watch out for these thieves.

They like to eat everything & aren't picky.

K is for Kick Boxing Heavyweight Rats,

They bounce off the ground like big acrobats.

Give them some space or they might start a fight,

I don't know which is worse, their kick or their bite.

L is for Lazy Tree Carpets with claws,
They hang from high branches without any flaws.
So soft & cuddly they rest & they doze,
Cute as a button from tail to nose.

M is for Milk Bears, so calm & serene,

They graze in fields, nibbling anything green.

With spots or patches like Dalmatian pups,

Making milk in their udders to fill up your cup.

N is for Nope Ropes, who wind through the grass,
They twist & they turn & they move really fast.
If they're not careful they get tied in knots,
Keep your eyes peeled during weather that's hot.

O is for Ocean Monsters with fangs,
The deepest blue waters are their domain.
With super sleek bodies, they cut through the waves,
If they ask you to hang out just say, not today!

P is for Piercing Shufflers, covered with jewels,
They love to accessorize & play by their own rules.
With tentative steps they move fro & to,
But don't sneak up behind them whatever you do.

Q is for Quick Nibblers, so small & bright eyed,
Looking through the house for new places to hide.
With the tiniest of paws, they nibble & play,
In search of munchies to start the new day.

R is for Rolly Polly Four Legged Knights,

All wrapped up in armor & ready for a fight.

With super strong shells to protect them from harm,

These cute little buggers are full of suave charm.

S is for Spark Butts up high in the sky,
Bugs with bright bottoms that glow as they fly.
Tiny winged light bulbs, they shimmer & shine,
Lighting the path from your home to mine.

T is for Trash Pandas looking for snacks,
Digging through trash cans & lost school lunch-sacks.
With masks on their faces, they sneak through the night,
Searching for goodies like chocolate & tripe.

U is for Underwater Spiked Balloons,

They puff up when they're scared like a floating full moon.

You may think they look silly, a little unreal,

But if you're in the ocean don't give them a feel.

V is for Vampiric Nocturnal Cave Birds,
They travel together, not saying a word.
Their favorite meals are always at night,
So when you're out camping stay cuddled up tight.

W is for Wobbling Tuxedos on Ice,

In perfect formation, they're very precise.

In their 3 piece suits, they waddle and play,

Slip sliding together the whole day away.

X is for Xanthic Long-Necked Tree Munchers,

With supersized legs they're tall limb & leaf crunchers.

Their necks stretched high to nibble & chew,

These interesting creatures always have the best view.

Y is for Yard Diggers, so full of glee,
They'll put holes in your socks with their claws & their teeth.
They're cute when they're sleeping & kissing your nose,
But can be real obnoxious when they pee on your clothes.

Z is for Zapping Underwater Umbrellas,
They look like they're dancing, on tiny propellers.
With tentacles trailing, they glide by with ease,
But if you get zapped, you'll be searching for pee.

about the author

Megs is a former child who's been obsessed with telling stories to her friends, family, pets & stuffed animals for as long as she can remember. After reading far too many boring books to her nephews while they were growing up, Megs has made it her mission to create engaging, amusing & entertaining children's books that are enjoyed by kids & grown-ups alike. For more information about Megs & to check out some of her other titles, visit her website @ www.megswrites.com.